G000036617

RICHARD NEWMAN

The 'It' Factor

*Your guide to unlocking
greater success in your business
and your personal life!*

Published in Great Britain 2009 by UK Body Talk Ltd

UK Body Talk Ltd.
121 Standard Road, Hounslow, Middlesex TW4 7AY
08451 30 70 99
www.ukbodytalk.com
info@ukbodytalk.com

Contents

Prologue

How the author correctly predicted the results of the 2008 American Presidential election, 15 months before the final votes, using the principles of the 'it' factor (with recorded proof of the prediction).

1 Introducing the 'It' Factor

Everyone wants it, few people have it, now you can learn it. Setting the scene for the skills you are about to learn and how they will help you succeed.

2 Are You On Top Already?

How close are you to having the 'it' factor? Measure your current skill level and discover the biggest mistake that holds most people back from achieving greater results.

3 Can You Feel It?

Find out how to harness the principles of global advertising to give you that extra alluring impact.

4 Your Personal 'Sip Test'

How to get chosen over your competitors, in business and pleasure, with lessons from some of the most successful companies and products in the world.

For my wife, who always had 'it'
and after all these years
has still got 'it'

Prologue

In September 2007 I was asked to go live on radio in Washington DC, on a political debate, to give my opinion on who would win the American Presidential race.

This was a daunting task for me. I don't follow politics and I didn't know the Presidential campaign had even begun. It was 15 months before the election would take place.

There were 15 Democratic candidates, 18 Republicans and another 40 candidates from other parties all hoping for votes. That's a grand total of 73 candidates to choose from. I was asked to talk about three of the candidates live on air. I watched as many videos of them as I could, to see each of them in action, speaking in debates and interviews. Then I gave the Americans my prediction, in a live broadcast from their capital city.

I spoke first about Hillary Clinton. At the time she had a vast lead over all the other Democrats. On one poll, she had 45% of the Democratic vote; a 30 point lead over the other candidates in her party, none of whom had more than 15%. She was going to be the sure fire winner, destined to be President, wasn't she?

I didn't think so. To me, every video showed she would lose.

Much as I had been looking forward to the idea of having our first ever female President of the United States, I was very disappointed by her communication style.

She is a highly competent woman, yet on every video I found, whether she was giving speeches or answering questions at a debate, she was trying too hard to sell her message. I felt her communication style was 'forced'

Her style showed a lack of belief in her ability to become President. She was constantly leaning forwards, raising her hands, with tension in her arms and thrusting her chin out as she spoke. This is much like a teacher you may have had at school - remember the type of teacher who lost control of the class and was desperate to get your attention, but didn't command the authority? That's a lot like how she appeared.

She may be a great politician and leader, but she didn't have the 'it' factor. As I said on air, I felt that her style was forced and that meant people would lose faith in her. Sure enough, they did. Her vast lead soon fell.

The next person we discussed was Rudy Guiliani. Having been Mayor of New York, and having guided the city and people through the events of 9/11, I felt he was in a good position to win votes. He was in fact the leading Republican candidate, with 21% of their support (1% ahead of John McCain, who went on to be the lead candidate for the Republicans).

However, when he was questioned about his stance on abortion and other issues he repeatedly stepped back, put his weight on his back-foot, pulled his chin in (which is a common sign of feeling vulnerable, subconsciously protecting your jugular vein from possible attack, by pulling in your chin) and he spoke with a defensive tone.

I said that it was my belief, based on these clips, that people would lose faith in him, as he appeared to be holding back and speaking defensively (something you would never associate with being 'Presidential'). Again, he is clearly a brilliant leader and has done great things for the Americans, but in those crucial televised moments he simply didn't have 'it'. As it turned out, he dropped out of the campaign very early on.

Two candidates down...71 more candidates to choose from. I had no idea who any of the other people were. I scanned through all the videos I could find to choose someone who looked and sounded like a leader.

If you haven't guessed yet, the third person we spoke about was a man who most people in the UK had never seen or heard of before. Barack Obama. As soon as I saw him on video it was clear to me he had 'it', but the radio show hosts completely disagreed with me. They criticised his policies and questioned his abilities. As I told them then, it wasn't just what he said that would influence people to vote for him. His success would come from his communication style.

Whenever he spoke he was standing centred, grounded and appeared in control. His gestures were broad and sweeping. He even made the classic 'thread-the-needle' gesture, which is where the tip of your index finger touches the tip of your thumb, as if you are holding a small thread. (This shows a sense of precision about your thoughts and ideas.) He wasn't making generic statements - he always looked like he had something specific to say. He looked like a leader. As I said live on air in Washington DC, 15 months before the election, when Obama was trailing 30 points behind in the polls, "this is the one to watch".

The remarkable thing about President Obama's campaign speeches is that very little of what he said can be remembered (apart from the simple phrase 'Yes We Can' which he apparently borrowed from Bob The Builder). He speaks intelligently about many things, but he didn't make famous statements that people could latch onto, such as:

> *"Ask not what your country can do for you, ask what you can do for your country,"* as John F Kennedy said.

Very few of Obama's words were memorable. They didn't need to be. He has something that all the other candidates lacked. He has the 'it' factor.

(If you're curious to hear the full interview you can find the original recording of this radio broadcast on our website.)

"Sometimes one creates a dynamic impression by saying something, and sometimes one creates as significant an impression by remaining silent."

Dalai Lama

CHAPTER 1

Introducing the 'It' Factor

Everyone wants it, few people have it, now you can learn it...

What Is The 'It' Factor?

Why would the person with the best CV get turned down for a job? Why do people buy second rate products from your competitors? How come the nicest person can't get a date? Most importantly... why don't people listen to you?!

It all comes down to that secret ingredient, the extra personal magic that helps you win the job, sign the deal, shine socially and make everything you say more magnetic and memorable.

The 'it' factor.

For years this magic ingredient has been talked about, yet shrouded in mystery. This book reveals proven techniques that are simple to follow and will instantly enable you to develop your own 'it' factor, so that you can have greater results in all areas of your life.

The Body Talk Training team have researched this book over 14 years, working with more than 10,000 people from 45 countries, including FTSE 100 companies, international celebrities, Tibetan monks and the UK Parliament, so you can rest assured that the techniques in here are proven to deliver reliable results for you, whatever your age, background, nationality or culture may be.

In today's competitive world this book will give you the extra edge you need to stand out from the crowd and get noticed for all the right reasons.

You're about to discover:

*   How to win authority and respect for your ideas, with examples taken from world leaders

*   Techniques used by famous brands in global advertising that will make you more persuasive and attractive

*   The vital, advanced body language and voice techniques that will instantly make you more compelling and memorable

*   How to express your true style confidently

*   The secret signals for reading people, so that you can have a greater understanding and connection with everyone around you

*   Straight forward advice for how to apply these skills to your life for immediate results

In the modern world people need to rely on their personal impact more than ever to win contracts, get hired, keep their jobs and impress clients, dates and colleagues.

People want to spend time and work with people who they like, respect and trust, all of which relies on that elusive 'it' factor. Remember, it's not always a logical decision to like or trust someone. It comes from something else. Either you've got 'it' or you haven't.

Fortunately, now you can learn 'it'.

This book is filled with techniques to increase your personal 'it' factor, to help you succeed in important situations.

You're not going to change who you are. Quite the opposite, in fact. This is about becoming who you really want to be.

Just to be clear, this book is also not about making you into the next 'it' girl or something equally shallow or superficial. Instead, it's about understanding how we connect with each other and allowing you to do so more powerfully, finding a deeper connection with the people you meet, and allowing you to reach your full potential.

These tips are easy to follow and if you put them into action pretty soon you'll be enjoying the results we've already shared in training events, speeches, VIP coaching and workshops, with many thousands of people across Europe, America, the Middle East and Asia.

Let's get started.

"We are what we repeatedly do.
Excellence then is not an act,
but a habit."

Aristotle

CHAPTER 2

Are You On Top Already?

How close are you to having the 'it' factor?

Before you start to learn the techniques and master the skills contained in this book, it's important to assess how good your current skill level already is. You may feel you already have a fairly high ability to communicate, but I can promise you there is something in here for everyone, even if you're among the highest achievers.

So to help you assess your progress along this journey use this simple list to rate how well you are doing now, according to how high you place yourself on this list, before we move on.

In terms of your communication skills, do you feel you are:

- In the top 1% of people
- In the top 10%
- Above average
- Average
- Below average
- Poor

Done it? If not, go back and do it now! This book will include lots of interactive elements that will be crucial to your success. This is simple, but it's important, so decide now.

How high do you currently rate yourself? Now I'm going to go way out on a limb here, as you and I may never have met before, but I'm going to bet that you placed yourself as being at least average (most likely higher!).

How do I know this? Well, as I learned from speaking to Richard van de Lagemaat, the author of the "Theory of Knowledge" (published by Cambridge University press) this survey was originally given to one million Americans, asking them to give their personal rating of their communication skills. Out of over one million people, how many do you think rated themselves as being 'average' or higher?

EVERY SINGLE ONE OF THEM.

Now, I'm not a mathematics professor, but that can't be right, can it? We can't all be above average. Roughly half of people must be below average in order for anybody to be above average.

That's not all.

When judging their communication skills:

> 60% rated themselves in the top 10%.

> 25% thought they were in the top 1%.

What does this all add up to?

Quite simply, it means that virtually everybody completely over-estimates how good they are at communicating (not just you!).

When you consider that communication is an essential survival skill, helping you to get a job and attract a mate, it makes sense that everyone is pretty good at this stuff. So the **average** ability is probably a lot higher than you thought. Therefore, in comparison to the average, most people are actually a lot lower on the list than they imagine

In our modern age 'survival of the fittest' is less about physical cave-man strength and more about a civilised kind of strength, such as being influential, engaging and entertaining. All of these attributes increase your personal attraction and earning potential, which in turn links back to our cave-man like needs to survive and re-produce.

This makes it that much more important for you to improve your skills in this area and to have the extra 'it' factor, to stand out from the crowd. Being brilliant, intelligent and wonderful on the inside simply isn't enough. You need to shine on the outside too.

Unfortunately, many people think they already have 'better than average' communication skills, which holds them back from becoming all they can be.

This is just like watching motor-racing on TV from the comfort of your sofa, such as Formula 1 racing, and saying, "I could drive better than that guy!" instead of recognising the extra skills that are required to make it look easy and the areas you need to work on to reach your full potential.

There may even be some things in this book you have heard about before, but unless you actually apply them in every interaction you can't class yourself as a great communicator.

> "To know and not to do is not to know"
> - Chinese proverb

So, be sure to practise every technique you come across, even if you think you've heard it before (although most things in this book will certainly be brand new information for you).

What do I know about this anyway?

I had the very fortunate experience to discover the 'it' factor and the essential ingredients for success while working in Formula 1 racing for five years.

I'm sure you've heard of Michael Schumacher. Even if you have never watched a race, you probably know his name because, among many achievements, he won five consecutive world championships for his driving, in the years 2000-2004, and seven world championships in total, making him a global superstar.

Now try naming who came second in those seasons. Even avid fans of the sport would struggle with that one.

In the world of Formula 1 sometimes new parts of the race car are developed over ten years, with many millions spent in research and development. During the racing season the cars are completely stripped of every component and rebuilt with new elements every couple of weeks...and when the car is finally produced, after all the effort and money involved, it can lose a race by 0.01 of a second, and become an 'also ran'.

Just like that, you could miss out on getting your dream job, perfect lover, or a life-changing deal over a tiny detail. You can work towards a goal for ten years, investing everything you have and miss out on success by a mere fraction.

You may never know what that tiny detail is that separates you between success and failure. That is, unless you get a life-changing opportunity similar to the one I did.

I was hired by the McLaren Formula 1 Racing team, which is the most impressive and focussed organisation I have come across. Working for them, I was able to practise changing tiny details in my communication skills, as I hosted meetings over five years, where I used the exact same script more than 1000 times, speaking to a vast number of the top executives in business from around the world, until I discovered a magic formula for communication success. Using the same words, I could get entirely different responses, by shifting my communication style by a small fraction.

I made a detailed analysis of what worked and what didn't, changing my style by smaller degrees, with the aim to achieve the best possible result.

Since then the 'it' factor has been shaped by 12,000 clients from 45 countries. This is something you can now learn, and re-create for yourself, in your own style, at any time. You can apply these techniques to business and social situations.

I'll be giving you the background strategies to begin with and then we'll move on to the specific techniques for success. First let's start with the foundation that the 'it' factor comes from, which I discovered by accident nine years ago.

"*You are not who you think you are. You are only what you communicate.*"

Derren Brown

CHAPTER 3

Can you feel it?

How to harness the principles of global advertising to give yourself that extra alluring impact.

It was September 2000 and the phone was ringing. It was my agent.

"I've got an audition for you!"

This was great news. After three years of intense acting school training in London and a few appearances on TV and in theatre I was keen for more work.

"Fantastic! What's it for?"

"Well, it's a bit different to normal...it's the McLaren Formula 1 Racing Team. They want to hire you to host their VIP meetings and deliver presentations for them."

This was strange news for an actor who was 'between jobs'. Usually my agent called with an audition for an advert, play or film.

It was even stranger for me because I had never watched a Formula 1 race, I had never given a business presentation of any kind and I had no interest in cars. In fact, two weeks before that phone-call I had blown up the engine on my car because I forgot to put water in it! The engine melted so much that the mechanics fell about laughing when they looked at it. So you can imagine my surprise when my agent offered me a job as a motor racing expert.

"Okay, fine, I'll go, but just answer me this. If they have 950 people working at their headquarters, all of whom know more about Formula 1, business meetings and presentations than I do, why would they want to hire me?"

"Because you're a communication expert! You can give them the extra personal impact they want. Now get your suit on and get down there."

Communication expert?

I'd never thought of myself that way. Now that I look back on things though, it did make sense. You see, I started my career in communication skills at the age of 18 by flying off to India. I went to live in the foothills of the Himalayas, near Darjeeling in a Tibetan monastery. I lived there for six months teaching the monks to speak English. It was my youthful way of setting out to change the world and do something good for others.

Well, when I arrived I discovered that the monks I was living with didn't speak any English. They spoke Tibetan, Nepali and Hindi. All I could speak was a bit of French and German, which wasn't going to be much help. In order to communicate with them I had to learn how to survive using a totally different language. Body language.

During my time living with the monks I was able to teach all of them how to speak good English and they even taught me how to speak Nepali back to them. It blew my mind how much we could communicate without the use of words. We formed a bond on a much deeper level. As you may know, the word 'rapport' comes from a Latin term that means 'non-verbally travelling together'. I experienced this in the most profound way, relying on non-verbal skills just to get through the day and communicate what I wanted.

When I came back to the UK I was determined to keep studying these skills and so I auditioned for acting schools. There were no degrees available in 'body language' and this seemed like the next best thing - to study communication.

Acting school is very different to what you may expect. Many people joke that you just dress up in tights and say "Thee!" and "Thou!" and get a diploma. The reality is that for three years we studied for 50-60 hours a week, learning how to breathe, how to sit, how to walk, how to move our arms, how to talk – studying how each movement and each breath would affect an audience.

My movement teacher called this 'non-verbal leakage' (a term used by one of the world's fore-most experts in this area,

Left: Richard with 'Paljor La', the head monk of the Zhekar Choedhe monastery, who always had a cheeky sense of humour.

Below: The monks enjoy a lesson in their kitchen, often with no electricity, working by candle-light to deal with the daily power-cuts.

Desmond Morris, zoologist and author of 'Peoplewatching') by which he meant the tiny changes you can make in your body language that have a profound effect on the people around you, making them feel differently about you. When I had to apply these skills to business, by working for McLaren, my life really changed. This time I wasn't going to be using what I'd learnt to be a compelling and engaging character on stage, or to teach monks. I had to use my body language and acting experience to become the most compelling and engaging version of myself in the world of big business, talking to companies such as Hugo Boss, Mobil and Mercedes-Benz, who gave millions of pounds worth of sponsorship to McLaren every year.

The task was made even harder by the fact that at the time McLaren were losing virtually every race to the Ferrari team and some chap who was doing rather well called Michael Schumacher. It was a tough time for them and it was crucial to make a good impression.

When I was handed a 20-page technical script about car manufacturing I knew I would have to apply everything I knew to bring it to life and be the best ambassador I could for their outstanding team.

Thankfully I stumbled across the answer.

The First Magic Ingredient of 'It'

My first ever business presentation started with learning a two-hour long script of technical information about cars. I had two weeks to memorise and perfect it before giving an important speech to a group who were being flown in from Germany. I wasn't allowed to use any notes. I just had to keep this audience of German engineers engaged with my expertise. I started this speech with a twenty minute introduction section, giving them the history about the racing team and the drivers. At the end of this section I paused briefly and, to my delight, I got a huge round of applause.

Wow, I thought, this is great! I kept going for the next hour and forty minutes, my confidence boosted by a good start and then I got another round of applause at the end.

I remember thinking, 'Fantastic, I won't get fired just yet!'

Then a senior member of staff came over to me, looking both concerned and surprised.

"What have you been telling them?" he asked.

Uh-oh, I thought, I've blown it.

"Well," I muttered, *"I just learned the script and delivered it to them, as you asked. That's all I've done."*

"Hmm," he said, looking confused, *"I've got to tell you, we've never had a round of applause at the end of one of these meetings, let alone at the beginning! You must have done something different?!"*

Suddenly it hit me like a ton of bricks. I had been applying the key principle to effective communication, which I had learnt as an actor. This is the first magic ingredient that makes all the difference between success and failure. It is something that every outstanding actor, singer and dancer uses to captivate you. It is potentially the most important element of show business, but it is often forgotten in the ordinary world of corporate business. Every time you communicate with another person you need to harness the power of this to have the most successful and powerful interaction, whether you are sending them an email, text message or meeting them face-to-face.

The world of advertising uses this simple principle to get you to buy products and services around the globe. Wouldn't it be great to use the same principle in your next job interview, sales pitch, presentation or date?

Here's how it works...

Ditch the fax machine approach

Recently we were working with a client on his communication style. I asked him how he wanted to come across in a sales pitch.

> *"It's just data transfer really. They want the information and I give it to them. Its technical stuff so there's no point trying to jazz it up."*

> *"Okay, well answer me this,"* I replied, *"If that were true, why are you even in the room?"*

> *"Huh?"*

> *"If you just need to give them the data you can do this by fax, email, post, text message, or phone-call. So if you're in the room with them, if they actually invited you to spend time with them, or perhaps they have even travelled to meet you, then they must want something more from you than 'data transfer'. So what is it?"*

He was lost. So are most people when I ask this question.

If people want data, send them an email. If they ask to meet you, you had better bring that data to life in a more interesting way than a fax machine. It sounds simple, and on a logical level most people understand this and apply it in their social lives, then they forget it when they go to work.

Whether it's a date, an interview or a sales-pitch, it's all the same. I'm sure you wouldn't show up to a first date and say;

> *"Look, I'm 30, I've got a secure job, my own home and all my own teeth, statistically I'm a very good catch for you, so what do you say...marriage?"*

It sounds silly when I put it like that, and yet people do this stuff every day in business meetings and many even do it with their kids, friends or families. They expect people to simply do things logically, treating them like machines and wonder what went wrong.

Whether it's business or pleasure you want to excel in, remember we are not human doings, we are human beings.

In his brilliant book, 'Predictably Irrational', Dan Ariely explains the hidden forces that shape our decisions. As a visiting Professor at MIT, one of the world's foremost academic institutes, filled with highly intelligent and logical people, he conducted experiments that prove in many ways that we act based on emotion, not logic.

For example, in one experiment he discovered that people feel greater pain relief from taking an expensive pain-killer, than from a cheaper pill (even though both pills used were secretly vitamin C pills, with different labels).

Perception creates your reality and determines your success, whether you are promoting a product, an idea, or yourself.

So in the technical age we live in, full of communication devices, the only possible reason for ever having a meeting with anyone face-to-face isn't because they want your data...it's because they want to *experience being with you*.

To be more specific, they want a couple of very important things from that experience with you, if you are going to be successful. These skills are becoming more important to your survival every day.

The Three Degrees of Separation – from man to machine

Think of it this way. Firstly, within just a few years most of us will have mobile phones with fast, reliable internet access. That means we will all be able to reach an almost endless amount of data on any subject we want at the push of a button, wherever we are. Secondly, with the current development in robotics and technology it is estimated that in just a couple of decades every job that can be automated will be. This means that if all you have to offer is data, or a systematic way of doing things, the value you offer an employer is about to become worthless. Luckily, humans can provide a few things that the internet and technology can't do (yet). Now, more than ever, it is crucial you become highly accomplished in these three areas.

What do humans have to offer that's different to all the things a machine can now provide? They are the very same things that make us valuable to each other:

1. Your ability to **communicate** your knowledge in a **more effective and engaging way** than a machine.

2. Your **compassion** and ability to make an **emotional connection** with other human beings.

3. Your ability to **apply** your knowledge more effectively and intuitively than machines can to any given situation.

What does this have to do with the 'it' factor? To put it simply, the greater you are at the above three things the more successful you will be. To make this even simpler for you let's get back to the McLaren story.

How did I use this information to take a script that had never received applause and get an overwhelming response time after time? Easy. The first thing I did was to apply the rules of 'KNOW, DO, FEEL'.

KNOW, DO, FEEL

Every time you speak to someone your brain will effectively ask you two questions, automatically. These questions are:

What do you want this person to KNOW?

What do you want this person to DO?

Let me give you an example.

Imagine you're telling a joke. What you want the other person to KNOW is the story of the joke. What you want them to DO is laugh. Everything you say, as you tell the joke, will come down to these two questions.

Imagine you're doing a sales-pitch. What you want the other person to KNOW is you are the best person for the job. What you want them to DO is hire you. Again, everything you say will come from these two questions.

Now let's take the example of the presentation I did at McLaren. What they wanted people to KNOW was the important facts about the team, how they were building and improving the cars to win more races and so on. What they wanted these sponsors to DO was to keep on sponsoring the team year after year, because this is how the company is funded. Everything in my twenty-page script (that I recited word for word) was based on these two questions.

All I did differently was to ask a simple, additional question, from a 'show business' perspective. As an outsider to the world of business and motor racing I couldn't help but ask myself the following...

> *"Okay, so these companies are paying millions of pounds every year to put a sticker of their company logo on a car that is being driven at 227 miles per hour (around 360 kph). That's like subliminal advertising... and the car's not even winning! Surely they could sponsor another sport, another team, or put their money into a whole range of different places. How can I help? I'd better make sure these people feel excited and inspired about working with McLaren!"*

And that in essence is the reason I got applause. It's part of the reason I was hired by the team for so long. It's part of the reason I went from being a shy kid to now making a very good living giving speeches, training courses and personal coaching to companies across Europe, the Middle East and America.

It's just related to a fundamental part of what makes us human. Anyone can have this effect, by using this principle.

In short, if you want to make a greater impact on the people around you, before you interact with anyone you must ask yourself...

How do you want them to FEEL?

As the saying goes,

> *"People will forget what you did, they will forget what you said, but they will never forget how you made them feel."*
> Maya Angelou

(Of course, when you've decided how you want someone to feel the next thing you need to know is exactly how to engage their feelings! Don't worry, I'll be explaining how you can do this in the coming chapters, once we have this foundation firmly in place.)

Why is this principle so important?

Maybe you're a very logical person, maybe you work in a very logical world, surrounded by logical people. So how does this apply to you?

Let's take an example we can all relate to...

Smoke gets in their eyes

In 2004 a 'Wonder Pill' made front page news in the Daily Mail, with claims that 'it stops you smoking, drinking and even reduces your weight!'

The article by the medical correspondent, Jenny Hope, went on to say that 13 million people in the UK were smokers and 10 million of them wanted to give up.

Two days later on the front page of the Metro newspaper was the headline of an article by David Harding stating, "Smoking causes half of all deaths!"

'Hmm,' I thought to myself, 'there's an open market here – I should run a seminar to help people give up smoking!'

Now just imagine that I had held a seminar for all 10 million people who 'wanted to give up smoking, but hadn't done it yet' and you are now standing in the front row. As you entered the arena you were given a photocopy of the front page of the Metro newspaper with all the statistics about how smoking kills many people, the dangers of smoking and so on.

Then I came on stage, with tremendous applause, and guaranteed to get you to give up smoking. What would have happened if I spoke like an average kind of communicator?

What if I was only using the two automatic questions of communication – thinking about what I wanted you to 'know' and 'do'. It might sound something like this...

> *"Good evening everybody! Now listen very carefully. What I want all of you to KNOW is that smoking causes half of all deaths and what I want all of you to DO is give up smoking. Thanks very much and good night!"*

That seems absurd, doesn't it? I mean no one would ever consider that to be effective communication, would they? Of course not. Most people do something much worse instead.

Many people who you meet every day in meetings or at parties will jabber on about what they want you to KNOW and DO for hours and then wonder why you stop listening, you don't take their advice or you just walk away!

Would this speech help people to give up smoking? No. Why not? Let me introduce you to the most effective and intelligent sales-force on the planet.

That's right... cigarette packets.

I'm sure you will have seen on all the cigarette packets these days messages saying things like **'Smoking kills'** or **'Smoking can cause a slow and painful death'** .

What would happen if you hung a sign like that around your neck that read:

'I will kill you – I may not kill you today, but if you keep hanging around with me for long enough I will eventually cause you to have a slow and painful death.'

Good luck getting a date or a job if you're giving out that kind of message! So why do ten million people still smoke, despite cigarette packets that actually say, 'Smoking kills – call this free-phone number to stop now 0800 169 0 169'.

What kind of sales force would ever expect to sell anything, when they are giving you the phone number to call in order NOT to buy the product?!

It is literally telling you what it wants you to KNOW (smoking kills) and what it wants you to DO (call the number and give up). And yet ten million people who say they want to give up still buy the packet and light up a cigarette. Why?

Well, according to the NHS Quit Smoking website when you smoke within seven seconds the nicotine hits your brain, giving you a natural high.

The rewarding feeling from cigarettes overrides the logic of quitting.

There are even leaflets available to help people stop smoking, published by a certain 'stop smoking' consultancy that tell you the benefits of giving up:

✓ Within 20 minutes of giving up your blood pressure and pulse rate will return to normal

✓ Within eight hours nicotine and carbon monoxide levels in the blood reduce by half

✓ After 72 hours bronchial tubes begin to relax

Zzzzzzzzzzzzzzzzzzz... telling people what they should KNOW is never going to help people quit smoking! (The cigarette packets are already telling them much worse stuff).

If logical messages aren't helping, what kind of message might work better?

In contrast to this logical message, in another leaflet by the same company (that is trying to help people quit smoking), they also tell you that:

'If you give up smoking you'll have an overwhelming FEELING of:

• Fear that you'll be giving up your only crutch or pleasure in life

- Fear that you won't enjoy life

- Fear that you'll put on weight

- Fear that you'll go through an awful trauma to get free

- Fear that you'll never be free of that craving feeling

That's five very powerful and painful feelings associated with giving up smoking! In contrast, by continuing to smoke people gain pleasurable feelings. In order to avoid pain and gain short-term pleasure people keep on smoking, even though logically they think they should give up. Their feelings override their logic.

In my opinion that's why ten million people who want to give up smoking don't give up, but don't just take it from me. Take it from science. Why are millions of pounds being invested into the 'Wonder Pill' (aka Acomplia) as featured on the front page of the Daily Mail? The aim of this pill is to change the way you feel about smoking and therefore when you take it you are far more likely to give up. (At the time of going to print this pill is still in development).

You may be wondering:

'How does this all relate to you and the 'it' factor?'

If you want to engage somebody in an interview, sales-pitch, networking event, date, at a party, presentation or speech you have to use both **logic and feeling.** So you should focus more on who you are 'being' rather than what you are saying.

Your words may be forgotten. The way people feel about you (and whatever you say) is what they will remember.

As I discovered teaching monks, training as an actor and speaking to executives for McLaren, if you can determine how people feel about you then you can have the 'it' factor.

The other crucial element I learnt while having to host one thousand meetings using pretty much the same script every time, is that how I used my body language and voice could totally change the emotional impact of the words, in more ways than you may expect.

In the now legendary experiments conducted by Albert Mehrabian in 1967, he found clues to the 'it' factor. His studies have been hugely misunderstood and misquoted over the years, so to put the record straight, what his studies showed is that we communicate fact and logic through words. However, when there is any inconsistency or lack of congruency in a person's communication style, the way we feel about someone, including their attitudes, words, statements and beliefs, is determined by:

7% words   38% tone   55% body posture

It is important to keep this study in the context it was intended for. It is also worth noting that Albert Mehrabian's studies are often criticised for having only 62 people involved, all of whom were women. So how valid is the data? Well, we have since conducted our own experiments with 8100 people, asking them how they feel when they hear a certain script of words. We then ask them what changes they would make to ensure the message is communicated more effectively. 8097 people have asked to change the person's body language and tone of voice, in order to make the message more successful. Only three people have asked to change the words.

This simply means that to be the most effective and powerful communicator you can be, your style must be congruent. Your body language, voice and words must all communicate the same message and emotion.

The challenge comes when you feel nervous, stressed, under pressure or anxious to perform well. These feelings create tension in your body, changing your body language and tone in such a way that ultimately damages and disrupts the way people feel about your words. It destroys your congruency.

Fortunately, you can use techniques that allow you to overcome the nerves and tension, to perform at your best and engage the right feelings in your listeners.

Remember that in order to impact the feelings of the people around you it isn't enough to simply 'feel it inside'. You will need to embody the appropriate feeling and share it. Or, as Dr Howard S. Friedman, distinguished

Professor of Psychology, found, you may need to shape up your A.C.T. (Affective Communication Test).

In my research to improve my own 'Affective Communication' ability I realised that by making small changes in my style, as I delivered the same words a thousand times, I could have a dramatically different impact on my results and the feelings of people around me, sometimes by shifting my body language by just one-inch.

By practising the techniques I learnt and developing much more affective communication skills, I was able to apply the 'it' factor to all areas of my life. I went from being single and broke, to marrying a wonderful woman and running my own business – a far cry from the time when I used to work twelve hours per day as a waiter. The skills I was lucky enough to stumble upon are all things that anyone can learn and benefit from.

Later on I'll explain exactly what actions you can use to help you achieve your goals, adjusting them to your individual style, using specific techniques.

Now though, it's time to understand the next powerful foundation concept, which you will need to build on to create your personal 'it' factor.

It's time to show you how the experts do it and how you can harness the magic created by global branding, without spending billions to achieve it.

Your personal 'it factor' is about taking everything you already have and making the most of it. Don't take it from me though, take it from the king...

My voice alone is just an ordinary voice. What people come to see is how I use it. If I stand still while I'm singing, I'm dead, man. I might as well go back to driving a truck.

Elvis Presley

CHAPTER 4

Your Personal 'Sip Test'

How to get chosen over your competitors, in business and pleasure.

Back in the early 1980s Coke made a terrible error – the type of error that you'll see people make every day in business and their personal lives.

You may remember the 'Pepsi Challenge', where people were stopped in the street and asked to try two drinks. They didn't know what they were drinking. They just had to say which they liked best. The majority discovered they preferred Pepsi.

Pepsi's market share began to soar. Coke began to panic. They conducted their own taste tests and discovered that people did indeed prefer the taste of Pepsi in these blind 'sip tests'. In fact 14% more people preferred Pepsi. That's equal to a phenomenal amount of money in terms of global customers. (For more details on this study check out Malcolm Gladwell's book 'Blink').

While you may remember the Pepsi Challenge you probably don't remember 'New Coke' – Coca Cola's answer to win more customers. They did extensive testing and decided to change the taste of Coke. They actually created a new taste that people liked better than Pepsi in these blind 'sip tests'.

Determined to win back market-share from Pepsi, they put 'new Coke' into shops.

Yes, that's right, the Coke you used to buy was replaced with a different taste.

Yikes.

There were protests. Petitions were signed.

Old Coke returned.

Coca Cola still has the market leading product, despite the fact that it has been proven in many tests that people prefer the taste of Pepsi. Why might this be?

In 2004 new tests were done to discover the reason. A new version of the Pepsi Challenge was run by Read Montague at Baylor College of Medicine. He also found that in blind taste tests most people preferred Pepsi. But. And this is a big but. When he told the volunteers what they were drinking before they tried the drinks almost all of them said they preferred the taste of Coke!

According to the brain scans used in these tests (called functional MRI scans) the volunteers had a reaction to Coca Cola in the part of the brain called the 'medial prefrontal cortex'. According to Edwin Colyer, a scientific writer based in Manchester, "This part of the brain is known to be involved in our sense of self. It fires in response to something - an image, name or concept - that resonates with who we are. Something clicks, and we are more likely to buy it."

This part of your brain is connected to the 'pleasure centre'. When stimulated, it enhances the feelings you have by releasing dopamine, increasing your enjoyment.

How can this help you? Simply put, if you want to succeed in business or your social life, as a parent, a husband or an executive, stop focussing on the contents of what you are talking about (your ideas, products, advice or knowledge) and start improving your delivery, packaging and personal brand.

This applies no matter how good your words are. Even if you think you have the best idea since sliced bread...

As Seth Godin reports in his great book 'Purple Cow', sliced bread was initially a complete failure.

People simply didn't buy sliced bread until they got the marketing right, through working with the 'Wonder' company...over a decade after it was invented!

So you might have the best company, product, service, or you may personally be the best thing since sliced bread, but even sliced bread needed to communicate its value effectively to become a success.

Coke makes all the right signals fire off in someone's brain, making them buy it, despite the apparently inferior taste. Their branding has the 'it' factor. You can have it too – any day, anytime, anywhere.

In summary of this principle, you can use techniques about how you present yourself everyday to help people feel the way you want them to feel about you or your company.

That's why people prefer the taste of Coke when they see the branding on the label. It's not the contents, it's the packaging.

That's partly why you chose the clothes you are wearing right now, the car you drive, your watch and the food you buy. You associate a strong feeling with those brands (such as this brand is safe, sexy, reliable, or good value) and therefore you buy them. For you, they have the 'it' factor.

In response to this, a lady once said,

> **"Oh, but I don't buy branded clothes.
> I just shop at Marks and Spencer's."**

Marks and Spencer's is a brand. So is Gucci, so is Primark. You have certain beliefs and feelings about what they will give you when you buy from them, from value to sex-appeal.

As the slogan goes, with melodic music and the seductive female voice lulling you into a feeling of luxury,

> 'It's not just food. It's Marks and Spencer's food."

Getting back to your personal 'it' factor. I hope you now have the sense that learning this and using the techniques that follow will be heaps of fun and in fact vital to giving you the extra edge in achieving all the success you want.

So forget the 'data transfer' method of communication. It's time to master your own style, taking all the lessons of the Pepsi Challenge and applying them to your personal goals. Stop worrying about the contents of who you are and what you have to offer for a moment. I'm sure that if you bought this book you're already a very intelligent, sophisticated, attractive and wonderful (not to mention discerning!) person, with great taste anyway.

You need to start focussing on your delivery, your personal 'it' factor. Think of it like a Christmas present. Why do we put them in fancy wrapping paper? It makes the contents more exciting. Why do women wear lingerie? Same answer!

So while you may be intelligent, sophisticated, attractive and wonderful if the packaging isn't right then nobody is going to be interested to find all the good qualities you have inside, or the great products your company has to offer.

The techniques that follow will help you present yourself to the world in the most effective way. They may feel unnatural at first, but pretty soon they will just be a part of your natural skill set, helping you create the impact you want and achieving the level of success you deserve.

"I pretended to be somebody I wanted to be and finally I became that person"

Cary Grant

CHAPTER 5

Let's Get Physical

Moving beyond the comfort zone to new behaviours

It's time to get cracking with some interactive bits that will put you on the road to success, with simple things you can do whenever you need to make the right impact.

Firstly, do this quick exercise. It will get you used to the kind of feeling you're going to experience for the next couple of weeks until you have mastered your own personal 'it factor'. In order to do this you will need to pop this book on your lap.

Go on, open the book out so it will sit comfortably at this page, keeping your hands free, set it down and follow the instructions. Do this now.

Put your palms together, then interlock your fingers.

Rest your thumbs on top. Notice which thumb is on top.

If your left thumb is on top it means you are more intelligent, funny and sexy (I'm kidding – I just want you to remember which one is on top - left or right?)

Now take your hands apart. This time you are going to do the same again BUT you are going to interlock the fingers differently, so that the other thumb naturally ends up on top. So don't just change your thumbs, you have to slightly alter the position of each of your fingers, so the other thumb ends up on top instead. Do it now.

Done it? Keep your fingers together like this as you keep reading.

Feels weird, doesn't it? It seems unnatural to keep your hands together in this new position, because the first way you did it was your natural preference. It's just the way you've always done it.

Now imagine if you sat like this in your next meeting, with your fingers resting on the table in the new position. Do you think anyone else would know that having your hands in that position feels different to you? Of course not! Plenty of people sit like that all the time.

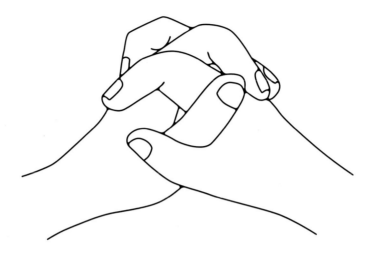

(You can relax your fingers now.)

That's how the rest of this book is going to feel. You'll be doing new things with your body and voice that will feel odd at first, but when you do them nobody else will know. These simple actions will instantly boost your 'it' factor and no one will know why, or be aware of what you're doing.

Unlike the thumb swapping exercise, the rest of the techniques I'll be sharing with you will allow you to get better results, both personally and professionally. All of these techniques are tried and tested with many thousands of past clients from around the world.

In some cases I'll be asking you to forget what you thought you knew about making a good impression and communicating. Sometimes I'll be asking you to do the opposite of what you've always been told.

You will also start noticing evidence of everything I'll be sharing with you, from the people you meet every day. You'll begin to understand why some people get a great reaction and why others fail, while you notice your own results improving.

Now that we've got the foundations in place we can move on to the specifics.

"The biggest problem with communication is the illusion that it has been accomplished."

George Bernard Shaw

CHAPTER 5

Vital Visuals

*How to get the MTV generation
to listen to you.*

A couple of years ago we trained a BBC news presenter how to deliver her news bulletins in a more powerful and memorable way. She was already very good, we just gave her the extra polish she wanted. Then she made a confession.

> *"I actually think my real problem at work is that people don't listen to my opinion in our meetings. We have these big boardroom discussions about our ideas for news stories, but the senior people in the room just won't listen to me. What can I do?"*

> *"Show me how you usually talk in these meetings,"* I suggested. *"What do you do? How do you say it?"*

She showed us.

> *"Oh, I see!"* I said, *"Don't worry, we just need to shift your style by a couple of inches and you'll get a very different result."*

Two weeks later we got a thank you card. She had just been promoted. What did we teach her? The six key elements of the 'it' factor.

It's important that you apply all 6 to get the best results, so we have devised a story to help you remember all of them.

It all comes down to the difference between being effective and being efficient. Whether you are giving advice to a teenager or a corporate boardroom, if you want to make an impact you need to be as effective as possible whenever you speak, instead of just being efficient, like most people.

To help you understand how this is done let me compare the way you deliver information to delivering food in a restaurant.

Let's imagine that this weekend you go to your favourite local restaurant for a nice hot lunch. I'm from England, so I want you to imagine that the special lunch of the day at the local Pub is "Bangers & Mash with onion gravy" (which is sausages and potatoes, for those of you who are not British, in case you're wondering!).

So you decide that you're going to have this and you take a seat and wait for the waiter to take your order.

Soon your very **efficient** waiter comes over.

>*"What can I get you?"* he asks very efficiently.

>*"Bangers & Mash with onion gravy please,"* you reply.

>*"No problem,"* he says.

Then he very efficiently runs to the kitchen to give the order to the chef.

The chef then very efficiently cooks up your food.

Seven minutes later it's ready (very efficient!).

The waiter efficiently runs to the kitchen to get your food.

As soon as the chef has finished cooking it the waiter scoops up the bangers & mash in his hands and comes charging out to throw the food straight into your mouth!

>*"What the hell are you doing?!"* you demand, with your face covered in hot food.

>*"I'm so sorry, I know what I've done wrong, I'll fix it right away!"* he says.

Then he very efficiently rushes back to the kitchen.

Ten seconds later he comes rushing back, very efficiently, with the bowl of onion gravy which he'd forgotten…

Just as he is about to pour the gravy over your head you shout,

>*"STOP! What is wrong with you? I want to see the manager!"*

"Of course," he says, and rushes off very efficiently to get him.

Very soon the efficient manager comes over to speak to you.

"Hello, is there a problem?" he asks.

"Yes!" you say, looking at the food that is now dripping off your clothing, "Can't you see that there's a problem?"

"Well," the manager replies, "you did order the bangers & mash?"

"Yes!" you tell him.

"And the waiter did bring you the food?"

"YES!"

You reply impatiently, pointing at the mess. The manager looks at you, very confused, before saying, "You mean to tell me that you came into my business, ordered my products and my service and you're still not happy!!!" he yells.

"Yes, that's right," you tell him, "but if I wanted sausages and potatoes I could have bought them at the supermarket and eaten them in the comfort of my own home. I don't need to come here for them. I came here because I wanted to enjoy the service, and atmostphere not just the food!"

And what did the waiter need to serve the food effectively? (I'll give you a hint - they are usually round and made of china). That's right - PLATES.

Now clearly I must have lost my mind - what on earth does this have to do with communication and the 'it' factor? Well, whether you are aware of this or not, you need to use your own personal P.L.A.T.E.S.™ to deliver information every day, in every interaction. Every time you speak to anyone it is totally up to you whether your words are delivered effectively or efficiently. You could just chuck them at people, like the waiter did, and hope for the best. You could talk in a logical, data transfer kind of way. Or you could give your words a really effective personal delivery by using your

P.L.A.T.E.S.™ - Posture, Legs, Arms, Tension, Eye-contact & Smiling.

These are the six physical elements of the 'it' factor, as demonstrated by BBC news presenters, Presidents, effective parents, teachers, sales-people and socialites.

The way that you use these six elements has a huge effect on how people respond to you. As I mentioned earlier, changing one of these by just one inch can totally change the reaction you get to anything you say.

So let's look at each of the six in detail.

"Constantly talking is not necessarily communicating."

Jim Carrey

CHAPTER 7

Personal Presence

Your posture is massively important for your state of mind, self-esteem and the first impression you make. Yet few people know how to use it really effectively to improve their personal impact, gain confidence and gravitas.

Let me give you an example. Imagine I told you that a person was feeling very depressed, down on himself, having a really bad day and generally feeling fed up with life? Could you guess what the man's posture might look like? Try it.

Did you guess that he might be slouched, slumped over, head looking down at the floor? Most people do, but whatever you guessed, the purpose of the exercise is to show you that if I tell you someone's emotion you can instantly guess what you think their posture looks like.

This works the other way around too.

Every time you look at someone's posture you will make a judgement about their state of mind.

I don't expect anyone to really walk around slouched over, looking at the floor. However, there will be certain things about your posture that you are unaware of, which create a specific impression on everyone you meet, in much more subtle ways than you imagine.

The way you use your body also affects your emotions and self-esteem. As discovered by Dr. Paul Ekman, who is considered one of the most eminent psychologists of the 20th Century, and a true master of human emotion (around whom the character Cal Lightman, of the FOX TV series 'Lie To Me', is loosely based) changing your body language directly impacts your emotions.

In fact, as his studies show, just by changing your facial expression you can change your heart rate and body temperature. So while your emotions may change your appearance, by controlling your expressions you can change your emotions. The two are intrinsically linked.

A lady said to me recently, "but isn't body language just superficial?". She couldn't be more wrong. It is a determining factor over how you feel and how others feel about you, therefore transforming the inner emotional experience and outward success you enjoy in your life.

Unless you come on a personal coaching event with us it will be hard for me to tell you exactly what shifts and movements may be most important for you. Until then, here are a few pointers to get you started.

People often ask me how someone like Anthony Hopkins or Judi Dench have such terrific presence and gravitas. How do they get that? Just take a look at what they do when they act.

They stand still and they speak. No gimmicks.
They just stand and speak...and it's brilliant.

The 'off-centre shuffle': most people stand off-centre, swaying from side to side, diminishing their visual impact and presence.

Where does this presence and gravitas come from then?

It's not their words. If you gave the same script to another actor the words would have a different impact.

It's not their clothing. If you gave their costume to someone else it wouldn't have the same effect.

Therefore it's not what they are saying or wearing that has this amazing effect. The 'it' factor comes from their specific actions.

When you watch them and listen to them, what they are doing with their voice and body creates a formula in your mind that makes you think 'wow'.

While I can't promise you an Oscar, if you can identify what actions consistently create this feeling you can of course boost your own personal impact.

How do they create such gravitas and presence? Part of this comes from something they do with their posture. They essentially do the exact opposite of what most people do.

Most people stand or sit in a way that makes gravity work against them. In contrast, part of the reason why the world's best speakers are so engaging is because they are using gravity to help them look and feel more powerful, authoritative and charismatic.

What most people do, whether they are sitting down or standing up, is they create anti-gravitas. As I like to call it, they perform the 'off-centre shuffle'.

This happens when you're sitting or standing. It is particularly obvious when someone is giving a speech or talking to a group.

As soon as they start they begin to sway from side to side. They put all their weight on one foot, leaning to one side...then they lean the other way... then they shift back to the first foot...and so on.

This rocking motion is something we are unaware of doing. It is designed to comfort us, like a baby being rocked to sleep. As you feel uncomfortable you re-create this sensation to comfort yourself. The biggest problem is that we are unaware of doing it, so this could continue for minutes or hours!

After about 30 seconds of swaying gently back and forth this will either make the people you are speaking to feel sea-sick, or it will make them feel hypnotised, watching the constant motion back and forth, as they began to feel very sleeeeeeeeepy!

This can continue for as long as they are talking to you, in conversation, at a party, a presentation, or a sales-pitch. It's like a pendulum swinging back and forth.

They may not realise why your conversation has suddenly become so tiresome to them, but they will lose concentration and tune out. They may assume that what you are saying is dull, when in fact your content is fine – the problem is your delivery, or more precisely your stance and posture.

Your body language should be attracting people to your words - not distracting them!

Why are these movements so unhelpful? Firstly, I am not suggesting that you should stand rooted to the spot whenever you speak. In fact, I encourage you to move. But…only move when your movements benefit the people you are talking to, never move just to make yourself feel better!

Remember, your body language is a language. These self-comforting movements create a distraction for your listeners and anything you say while you're swaying will lose its impact. It's a bit like trying to watch TV while the radio is on! If you want to allow people to really focus on your words you must focus on your movements and ensure they reinforce your words, not distract from them.

But what about gravitas? If you shift around and put all your weight on one foot you will be standing off-balance and if someone pushed you gently you would easily fall over. Ever wonder why some people are called a 'push-over'? It refers to people who do not look physically commanding and who could easily be pushed over.

We associate this phrase to describe the strength of a person's opinions, when really it is something that we pick up on from their posture and balance.

Therefore you can transform the impression people have of your opinions just by changing your posture!

Ideally, to have gravitas you need to be centred and free from unnecessary tension, with a slightly lifted sternum, giving the outward appearance that you have something important to say. Just like Christmas wrapping paper or lingerie, it makes what you have to offer on the inside far more appealing!

Remember, the 'it' factor is not purely about your appearance and your actions. You need to have something interesting to say too. The 'it' factor is about helping the people around you appreciate all the good things you have to offer. Avoiding swaying, bobbing and resting on one hip allows you to have more gravitas and bring your words to centre stage.

The 'it' factor will open the door to make it seem worthwhile for people to take a chance on you, be open to your ideas and respond more positively when you speak.

If you start to apply these techniques about your posture you'll be on your way to boosting your own presence.

That's the 'P' P.L.A.T.E.S.™ covered for you. That's just one of the six elements, and the magic really starts to happen when you play around with all the ingredients and find out how you can mix and match them together. Once you have the basic essence of each part in place you'll see it all in action.

Now let's move on to the 'L '– for Legs!

"My legs aren't beautiful, I just know what to do with them."

Marlene Dietrich, Hollywood Idol.

CHAPTER 8

Fatal Distraction

Why aren't you listening to me?

When I teach negotiation skills at workshops and conferences I often include a live lie-detection contest, with people in the audience competing against each other. They choose to either tell a true story or a lie and the rest of the audience have to guess who they think is lying.

Most people get it wrong, because they are looking for all the wrong signals. Here's my quick tip on this. If you want to know if someone is telling the truth, don't look them in the eyes. Instead look at their legs. When we are lying we become very aware of what we are doing with our face and our hands. Liars don't tend to consider their leg movements at all important, so it is more likely to find signals and movements here. This is also true of people who are simply anxious, nervous, or wanting to make a good impression.

While the top half of your body may be under control, the bottom half can give away your nerves and destroy the power of what you are saying. These movements are fatal distractions from your words and overall impact.

Remember, no matter how nice your legs are, this is not where you want people to be looking while you're talking!

There are several major causes of distraction...

Pacing - Have you ever watched someone wandering backwards and forwards while they were talking, giving a speech, or over coffee at networking events, or in a meeting? Perhaps they took a few steps forward when they had a new point to make and then took a few steps back?

The very fact that you noticed this shows how distracting it was. You may not have realised it at the time, but all of these movements were using up your precious concentration. They were taking your mind away from the person's words.

These movements are known as "fight or flight". This is a caveman instinct that we all have to protect us from situations that make us feel anxious or in danger.

What is this instinct for? Imagine a caveman living in the jungle and he hears a loud roar in the distance. His natural instinct will tell him he has two choices – he can stay and fight, or take flight (by running in the opposite direction).

You still have the same instinct hard-wired into you today. When you feel anxious, in danger, stressed or nervous this caveman impulse tells you that you have a choice - you can stay there and fight the danger (i.e. try to overcome the nerves by stepping boldly forwards and facing the situation) or you can take flight from the situation that makes you anxious (i.e. run screaming out of the building!).

Of course, you know that running away from the situation isn't going to win you any respect, whether you're doing a sales pitch, or lecturing a teenager, so you will only get a few steps back before your 'fight' instinct kicks in and you step forwards again, unaware consciously this is going on.

The "fight or flight" instinct can keep you moving back and forward for minutes or hours, the whole time you are speaking at a party or when giving a speech, because you don't want to be there, but you know you cannot run away.

This creates pacing.

You might say,

"But I like pacing, I think on my feet..."

Like I said before, if you want to make a great impact on people you need to consider which actions will be best for your message and your audience, rather than simply using your body language to make you 'feel better'.

Your body language is for other people, not for you.

This is just like any other language. Saying 'Scooby-dooby-doo!' every five seconds may feel nice to you, but unless it's relevant to the people you interact with it would be pointless saying it. It's just an annoying distraction.

So are comforting body language movements. They are both languages and should be treated as such for powerful communication.

If you move your body in a way that simply feels nice for you, pacing around, it will be a fatal distraction from your words and the message will be lost. (I am not saying "don't move", but move when you have a reason to move. Move if it benefits the person you are talking to or re-enforces your words).

You may be sitting there very confidently now, thinking, 'This isn't relevant to me. I don't pace.' Well, if you think you don't pace chances are that you probably do, without realising it! Most pacers won't believe it until shown a video as proof. As your legs are out of your direct eye-line you find it harder to remember any movements you make in this area. Sadly, the people around you will notice, even if you don't, and be distracted by it, so it's best to ask someone for feedback on whether you do it or not, otherwise you may never know.

You may also be thinking,

> **"This doesn't relate to me, I never speak to groups, therefore I would never pace around."**

However, if you don't pace you may be guilty of bobbing.

Bobbing

You will have seen this action performed by countless people around the world. Parents do it, sales-people do it, directors do it...it happens everywhere - at the water cooler, at a bar, in a sales-pitch, in an interview, wherever people want to make a good impression. And this bobbing movement destroys your 'it' factor.

Bobbing is the smallest version of pacing. The back and forth motion simply happens on the spot. I'm sure you've seen people who bob up and down when they talk to you. Usually they bob up

THE 'IT' FACTOR **69**

at the beginning of a new point they are making, or during a silent moment when they feel slightly uneasy.

Now you may be asking...

"But what's the big deal about bobbing?" So you bounce up and down occasionally. So what? Well, think about it. When you are bobbing you are once again off-centre, off-balance and you will look like a push-over. This may be helpful if you are doing your best not to intimidate someone, like a small child or a nervous new employee, but it will take away your authority, gravitas and presence.

The reason that leg movements are a fatal distraction can be simply explained like this. When you move and talk at the same time people have to process your movements and words at the same time. If your actions have nothing to do with what you're saying then it's a bit like this...

"Imagine I was telling you LEGS a quick LEGS story and LEGS after every LEGS couple of LEGS words I added another LEGS word that had LEGS nothing LEGS to do with LEGS the story. You'd have a pretty hard time understanding what I was saying!"

That's what it's like for people who listen to you when your legs are moving. They are processing your language as well as your body language, to decipher your message. Therefore it's best to make sure these two languages work together.

This applies even when you're sitting down!

You may think this only applies if you're standing up, but no! Even if you are sat behind a table or desk, where no one can even see your legs, they can still be a distraction. When you're sitting down any leg movements mean that the top half of your body will jiggle around. This means that people who are looking at you will think they are looking at Elvis, but only getting the top half!

Your brain is like a radar. It draws your attention to things that it feels are important to you. Specifically I am talking about a part of your mind called the Reticular Activating System (or RAS), which is constantly looking out for things that may be important.

For example, have you noticed that if you buy a new car you suddenly start seeing lots of other people driving that same type of car? Before you bought it you may not have noticed them at all. That's because your RAS didn't consider those cars important before. Now they are on your radar.

According to research, there are over two million bits of information available at any given moment that your brain could focus on. However, your brain can only process about seven pieces of information at once (the average being five to nine bits of information a person can process). Your RAS has to choose which seven are the most important elements to you in each moment.

Try this…I want you to focus on your underwear. Feel the sensation of it against your skin (if you're not wearing any, shame on you and stop reading while you're naked!). But seriously, focus on the sensation of your underwear. Notice the texture, how tight or loose it is and feel it comfortably resting against your skin. Now ask yourself this - were you aware of these feelings before I asked you to focus on them? No. Not unless they are particularly tight or itchy (and if they are itchy you might want to go and change, as I need your full attention!). The point is that the sensation of your underwear against your skin was already there, but your RAS just chose not to focus on it, as it was deemed to be unimportant, especially if you've worn that type of underwear many times before. Your mind knows it is safe and irrelevant to focus on.

How can you use this to your advantage? Remember that people can only focus on about seven pieces of information. This means that any distracting movements you make will take people's focus away from your words.

Imagine for example that while you are talking you are…

1) Pacing
2) Scratching your head
3) Speaking with a shaky tone of voice
4) Waving your hands wildly around
5) Finding it hard to breathe calmly, so you stumble over your words or don't articulate clearly
6) Speaking with a strong accent, or a quiet voice
7) Feeling tense, in a way that may be visible to others

Ding, ding, ding! Bingo! That's a full house. Suddenly people are no longer able to focus on your words at all, because there are too many distractions in the room.

There are many more that could happen, such as the room could be too hot or too cold, they may be hungry, thirsty, tired, you may be wearing a very interesting outfit that catches their attention, they may find you very attractive or unattractive (don't worry, that happens to all of us!), they may be making notes, or they could be distracted by other people moving around them.

As criminologist David Klinger explains, in his book 'Into The Kill Zone', when we are in extreme situations our senses shut down and we get a kind of tunnel vision, with heightened visual clarity and diminished sound. In important business negotiations, or life-changing personal or professional moments we have all felt under pressure to make the right choice. You need to make sure in these crucial situations that you are giving the right visual message, as it will be far more important than you may have imagined.

There are plenty of things that you cannot control about keeping the attention of the people you meet every day. But there are many more that you can control.

Whatever happens, make sure your body language and voice are attracting people to your words, not distracting them.

May be your wondering "Hang on a second, are you saying that the 'it' factor is all about being still?"

No. If you keep your posture centred and only move your legs when you have a reason to move them, then you could still be really dull!

We learn from what we hear as well as what we see, so the people you interact with need you to engage other parts of your body to make sure you are interesting enough that they simply 'can't take their eyes off you'.

The best way to do that is to use the next vital visual as we go through the 'six key elements'.

We've done 'Posture' and 'Legs', now it's time for the 'A' in P.L.A.T.E.S™...which is where you can really discover your style, your expressive freedom and your personal 'it' factor.

"A look, a gesture, which to everybody else is insignificant, tells you more about a man than words can."

Henry David Thoreau

CHAPTER 9

Armed & Ready For Action

The key to being visually engaging is gestures. You may have some worries about this. You might think that you are too shy, nervous or business-like to wave your arms around. You may even think these movements are a little eccentric or unnecessary. Quite the contrary.

Gestures are vital for helping you express what you say. They stimulate your memory and reinforce your message.

In 2004 there was a study done at the University of Chicago that proved this. They presented mathematicians with a memory test. Half of them were encouraged to gesture as they gave their answers. Half were not allowed to gesture at all. Those who gestured had results which were 10% better.

Their memories had been stimulated by moving their arms.

According to the psychologists, using the body during speech improves the brain function of the speaker, making them better communicators.

As Dr. Susan Golding said,

> *"It helps mental coherence and increases the efficiency of speech. The movements are not 'hand waving'. They are closely related to thought processing in the brain."*

Keep in mind that this study was done on mathematicians, who are not exactly known for using big, expressive gestures all the time! So we're not talking about an unusually expressive group here. Just normal, average people, showing that gestures are terrific for your memory, thought processing and mental coherence when you speak.

That's all very well, but how can I prove this to you? Well, I'm sure that at some point you will have seen a quiz show like "Who wants to be a millionaire?" There is a lot of money available to win for answering a few questions. Something that often happens on these shows is that the contestants will be doing very well until the jackpot of money gets higher. Then they start to get anxious, tense and they freeze up.

In the case of "Who wants to be a millionaire?" in the UK the presenter is Chris Tarrant, and when the contestant starts to look worried this is what usually happens next...

> The contestant says, *"I don't know what the answer is, Chris."*
>
> He replies, teasing them, *"I bet you know it really. If you were sitting at home watching this show you'd be yelling the answer at the screen, wouldn't you?"*
>
> *"Yes, Chris. I probably would,"* they say, *"but I just can't remember it!"*

What's the big difference between sitting in the TV studio and sitting at home? In the TV studio they are sitting there thinking "I'm on national TV, I don't want to look stupid in front of everyone who knows me" while they get more and more anxious and tense about the money.

They have lost their congruency.

You can bet that the people who are watching the show at home are waving their hands at the screen saying, *"I know the answer! It's so obvious!"* they cry, flailing their arms about, *"I should go on this show!"*

By having congruency and using expressive gestures at home it allows their thoughts and memory to flow much more easily, naturally and free of unnecessary tension.

This is great news for you. When you are the focus of a group of people you need to be visually engaging, to hold their attention. You also need to stimulate your memory to help your flow of thoughts come out naturally. By using your arms effectively you achieve both.

WARNING!

This is where we could get into real trouble! When I say to clients that they should make themselves more visually interesting by using their arms, I often get more from them than I expected.

I will say this just once. Gesturing is not charades! Gestures are for emphasis. They reinforce what you say. They are not supposed to act it out for you!

Gesturing is designed to help to emphasise your words and provide a visual guide to your meaning, giving your message greater emotional impact.

For instance, some of the clients I train think that 3% is an important amount. For others this is quite a small amount. So when they are doing a presentation involving numbers they need to show how they feel about 3%. Is it big or small? Is it important or not? Your body language and tone will tell us.

For example, I was working at a medical conference in Madrid. The top medical experts from across Europe and the Middle East were gathered there to discuss a new treatment for cancer. My team had the responsibility of coaching each of them on their presentation style, to ensure they spread the message about this treatment.

I explained to them that if they gave a talk about this new treatment, making small, shaky gestures, then the reaction in the audience would be to shrug their shoulders as if to say 'so what, it's only 3% better than the rest, it doesn't seem important, the evidence isn't solid' and keep using the old treatments.

However, if they gestured with wide, strong movements, with their hands far apart as they said "3%" then the audience would believe it to be more significant. This is even true of the top medical figures around the world. This is a field we work with extensively. You may feel that they will simply make decisions based on fact and logic, but the way someone feels about your facts and logic is related to the way you present the information to them.

So remember, when you discuss facts they only have the meaning that you give them. Words are just facts. How people respond comes down to how you make them feel.

Is 3% big or small? You decide.

The Cracked Record

Now that you get the idea that gestures are important, you could fall into the trap that many people suffer from - using a gesture you really like over and over again!

I'm sure you've seen people who talk to you waving that same finger, or the same hand in the same way...again and again. We all have habits like this - a certain body language pattern that feels very comfortable and we do it without realising.

If you make the same movements over and over people will once again be distracted away from your words. They'll just end up thinking "Stop moving your arm like that!"

Their brain simply wants to escape this rhythm. It needs variety. We all do.

So we need to add a few more gestures to your repertoire. Let's begin with the two most powerful, effective and simple gestures you can use every day.

These are two gestures that you use all the time. Up until now you may have been totally unaware of using them and the effect they have.

I'm in charge vs. You're in charge

The best way to understand this principle is to imagine shaking hands in three different ways. I'm sure you can shake hands perfectly well (that's not what this is about), this is simply the best way to remember this principle:

Firstly think about the **angle of your hand** in a handshake.

- Imagine shaking hands with your palm facing downwards. Keeping your wrist straight, you put your hand firmly out in front of you. Imagine how it would feel for the other person.

- Secondly, imagine shaking hands with your palm facing upwards. How would this feel?

Thirdly, focus on your **other hand**

- Imagine shaking hands normally, but adding your other hand on the person's wrist, or their arm, or their shoulder.

How would these handshakes feel? What effect would they have on the other person?

The clients we have coached across many different countries and cultures agree that shaking hands 'Palms Down' feels dominant and 'Palms Up' feels submissive.

They also say that using two hands has added warmth, but you wouldn't shake hands like this with a stranger.

Do you agree? You probably do, but if not be aware that these are the feelings that the vast majority of people will take from these handshakes, so you may want to consider that when you shake hands!

But what does this have to do with the 'it factor'?

You may not shake hands with every one you meet. However, **your gestures have the same physical impact on people when you speak to them as handshakes do.**

When you gesture 'Palms Down' it creates completely the opposite effect to gesturing 'Palms Up'.

Using a **second hand acts as an amplifier** of the feeling you create, just as it would in a handshake.

How does this translate into gestures?

Imagine you are telling a group of people some important information. When you get to the end there is an awkward question asked by a person in the audience (I'm sure you've seen this happen before).

> Perhaps the person asks you, "Are you sure these facts and figures are correct? They sound wrong to me. *Are you absolutely certain?!*"

You have several options for what you could do next. You could try...

Version One
(Palms Up, with a shrug) "Err...I'm sure these facts and figures are correct...

(Palms Down) ...Do you have any other questions?"

Or...

Version Two
(Palms Down, confidently) "I'm sure these facts and figures are correct...

(Palms Up, relaxed) ...Do you have any other questions?"

Which one of these options feels stronger to you? Which one makes you sound confident about your statistics and open to answering any questions? You probably agree that version two gives the more confident impression. But why?

When you use the gestures in version one you effectively look like you are saying...

> (Palms Up) *"I have no idea what I'm saying, I relinquish responsibility, it's not my fault!...*
>
> (Palms Down) *...Don't ask me any other questions!"*

In contrast, version 2 looks like you are saying...

(Palms Down) *"I am totally certain that these facts and figures are correct ...*

(Palms Up) *...I'm open to any questions you have."*

So remember...

• 'Palms up' is for open statements such as *"What do you think?"*

• 'Palms down' is for closed statements, such as, *"I am certain about this".*

• Two hands act as an 'amplifier' to each emotion, strengthening the impact

"You had them in the palm of your hand!"

Play around with these and see how much impact they have on the way people respond to you. Use 'palms up' to invite a response from the person you are talking to, or when you introduce yourself. This will help to make you look open, relaxed, friendly and confident. Use 'palms down' to emphasise closed, definitive statements. This shows that your decision is final. Use two hands to reinforce the message.

As a great example of this, let's go back to the story about the BBC news reader who we worked with.

I asked her to demonstrate how she usually spoke in meetings. She sat back in her chair (losing her gravitas instantly by being off-centre) and gestured with her hands palms-up. She was sitting like a push-over and her gestures were giving people an open invitation to say 'no' to her suggestions.

Richard puts on his serious face, along with palms down to show 'this is my final offer!'

We coached her to: pull her posture up from her sternum, so that she sat centred with her feet flat on the floor,... and gesture 'palms down'.

Afterwards she said that she felt much more confident, people had noticed a difference in her and her ideas were being taken more seriously. Mission accomplished. All by shifting her body language by about two inches and flipping her hands over the other way.

That's how important body language is. Changing one inch can make all the difference. You just need to know which bit to shift and why!

Let's have a quick recap on gestures. They:

- Stimulate your memory

- Speed up your thoughts

- Add emphasis to your voice

- Make you visually interesting

- Reinforce your message.

People learn from what they hear as well as what they see.

Therefore it is crucial to gesture to hold people's attention, keep your mind focussed and add impact to your message.

If you want someone to be visually excited by you, using a variety of gestures that match your message will help you achieve this (especially when you have practised for a while and allowed these techniques to become part of your natural style). Whatever you want someone to feel, it is vital that you read on to the next section. If your posture, legs and arms are all doing wonderful things you can still lose your personal 'it' factor unless you get the right balance with the 'T' on P.L.A.T.E.S...the one element that makes all the difference.

"The way we communicate with others and with ourselves ultimately determines the quality of our lives"

Anthony Robbins

CHAPTER 10

Creating Natural Charisma

The 'T' in P.L.A.T.E.S™ is for Tension. If you are standing centred (to gain gravitas), with your legs planted confidently (to keep people's focus on your words) and you're using gestures to reinforce your message (to gain charisma)...tension could still destroy all of these qualities.

Adapting your style to the people you meet is crucial to your success. If you want to learn more about reading people and interpreting their signals you may want to come on a training course with us. For now though it's important to make your style adaptable, rather than rigid.

Tension isn't all bad though. Positive tension makes you look exciting. You need a certain level of tension to make your gestures strong and confident. If they lack tension they will not have enough energy to carry the right message. On the other hand, a lot of unnecessary tension will make you uncomfortable to watch and listen to. Getting the balance right is the big key.

When all of your resources are working fluidly together as you express yourself you have *natural charisma*. We have all had this at some point, but you may be unaware of how to harness your charisma when you really want to use it for important personal or professional situations.

The definition of charisma is *"The ability to develop or inspire in others a commitment to a particular point of view."* That sense of absolute commitment is created by your congruency, through your body language, words and voice working together. **You can only reach this if you are in control of the tension in your body.**

Just think of a time when you saw a friend telling a great story and everybody was hooked, waiting to hear the ending, or a comedian told a terrific joke, or a presenter held you spellbound with his captivating ideas.

I'm sure you will agree that if you had given those exact same words to someone else it is possible that they could have sounded dull. It was the delivery that made it exciting. You may not have realised it, but any time that a person has this charismatic effect on you they are using congruency, either naturally or because they have been taught how to do it.

Now you might say, "It can't be this difficult, surely I have congruency anyway? If I'm not lying then my body language, voice and words should all be heading in the same direction, so I have congruency!"

> *That's absolutely true.*
> *We all have congruency.*
> *On the weekends.*

When we are relaxed in our own environment, perhaps at home or in the pub, on holiday, seeing our friends or playing with our kids, we all have congruency. However, we lose this congruency when we are in a situation that makes us nervous, anxious, under pressure or stressed in some way. Perhaps you feel anxious about certain deadlines you are working towards, or stressed by certain people you have to deal with, or nervous about a sales-pitch, presentation or meeting you have coming up soon.

Anxiety, stress, pressure and nerves create tension in your body.
This tension destroys your ability to be congruent.

We have all seen somebody stand up to give a speech who looked nervous (or perhaps petrified!). Suddenly, they were no longer the chatty, expressive person you know them to be. Did you notice that they moved a lot less, perhaps their voice sounded thin and their face lacked the normal level of expression? This is all due to tension.

When we are in a situation that makes us even a little bit stressed our bodies get tense and we cannot communicate as effectively as when we are relaxed with our friends. One of the most important keys to being a more confident presenter is to get rid of this tension. Quickly!

Interactive Exercise - 'Instant calm'

Let me show you how…

We used to teach a long tension releasing exercise. Then we worked on a conference in Prague with some of the top experts in psychiatry from around the world. They showed us a very simple exercise they use to help psychiatric patients feel calm, energised and positive.

Again, it may feel a little unusual when you do this exercise, but it is so effective. This is something I do if I am getting nervous before a big speech, or even in the middle of the day when I'm working hard towards an important project.

It releases all the unnecessary tension in your body, leaving you feeling fresh, relaxed and ready for action. This is just what you need to shake any final worries before you deliver an important speech, presentation or interview.

So close the door, ignore the phone and take yourself slowly through this exercise. Make sure you take it easy the first time. You will soon get used to it and be able to do it faster, but take it slowly at first to learn the routine. Take your time and follow these instructions carefully...

The Bunny

- Sit in your chair, with your back straight (staying as relaxed as you can)

- Put both arms out in front of you, pointing straight ahead

- Clench both fists tightly

- Keep your knuckles clenched as tight as you can the whole way through the exercise to feel the most benefit

- Keep your arms straight out and slowly push your knuckles down towards the ground - you will feel tension build in the muscle on the under-side of your arm

- Keep everything the same, but turn your arms to face up, so your knuckles are now pushing upwards, your arms still

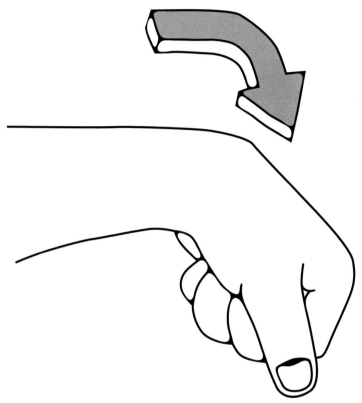

straight - you will feel tension build on the other side of your arm

- Now bend your arms in towards you, as if you are flexing your biceps. Feel the tension grow in your bicep.

- Keep everything the same, still clenching the fists and pushing the knuckles down, but now turn your fore-arms around, so that they are facing away from you. You will feel the tension in your triceps this time. (The back of your upper-arm).

- Keep it all the same, but raise your shoulders as high as you can, feeling the tension build in the muscles between your neck and shoulder

- Now lift your feet off the floor

- Keep everything the same, but now also flex your feet.

- Now quickly scrunch up your face as much as you can. Do it now.

- You should now look roughly like this…

- Now really scrunch up every area - fists, shoulders, feet and face

- And on the count of 3 let it all go **as you stand up and blow out, releasing all the tension**

- 3, 2, 1, *Release it all!*

How did that feel? Did you have a wave of tension leave your body? If not go back to the exercise and do it all again. It's really worthwhile getting the hang of this, because when you have a tense situation facing you and you've got just 30 seconds before you begin, this is one of the exercises that will work wonders to ensure your success (I'll be giving you some more later on).

I do the above exercise in about ten seconds, and yes I do always find a private spot to do it! Either my office or the nearest toilet cubicle (a bit like Superman preparing for a mission, but without the cape and blue tights).

This is one of the exercises that people find useful for everyday use when they are feeling anxious, as well as for the most crucial situations. You may not feel the full benefits of it now, but you certainly will the next time you feel stressed!

Creating the right level of tension in our bodies is vital for being able to use our body language and voice effectively.

Now that you have released that destructive tension you will be ready to gain the most benefit from all the other skills.

Remember, just a few small changes make a big difference.

Changing your body language by just one inch can completely transform your personal impact and the way people respond to you! Releasing tension has a subtle yet powerful effect.

And now it's time for the 'E' in P.L.A.T.E.S.™ ...

*"Small is the number of people
who see with their eyes
and think with their minds."*

Albert Einstein

CHAPTER 11

Basic Instincts

Eye-contact is so important to us in any interaction. We all have very primitive associations with eyes. They are the first things we begin to recognise after we are born. We are so affected by this that you can even cheer up a baby aged up to three months old by showing them two big black dots, which they will associate with their provider of love and affection (as discovered in the studies performed by P.H.Wolff in 1963).

Besides this, if you are giving any kind of presentation, speech, interview or having a meeting then it is crucial to have plenty of eye-contact. Otherwise why bother meeting them? Think about this…

Anything that you say in a meeting could be said on the phone.

Anything you give people could be sent in the post.

Power-point can be e-mailed around the world instantly.

Therefore, if you meet anybody, anywhere at any time, the ONLY reason you are there is to have face-to-face contact with them.

This means that eye-contact and the effect of your overall body language impact on each other is absolutely vital.

It is the only true purpose of any meeting.

With this in mind I should make you aware of one small but important point. If you make eye-contact with someone for more than about three seconds they will start having a reaction I have labelled 'Kiss or Kill', meaning as a simple cave-man like response to extended eye-contact they will:

- Stop breathing
- Look away
- Do both of the above
- Assume that you are attracted to them, or planning to attack them.

The reason for this 'kiss or kill' response is simply that you only usually give extended eye-contact when you want to kiss or kill someone. It's not natural. Unfortunately, some people think that eye-contact is so important that they never look away, making them appear intimidating and unnatural.

The actor Sean Maguire was once quoted as saying that after many years working on popular TV shows he was amazed at the response to his first music video. Suddenly women were throwing themselves at him, infatuated with him! What was the difference? For a decade before that he had been working on soaps, then when he did a music video his eye-contact had shifted. He was looking straight at the women who were watching, giving them extended eye-contact (although gyrating his body to music may have also helped!).

So remember, if you want people to feel relaxed around you make eye-contact in relatively short, relaxed bursts. You will naturally do this most of the time. However, when you are in a stressful environment it's not always easy to remember how you naturally behave. This is your easy reminder for keeping your eye-contact natural and relaxed.

On the other hand, you may be someone who struggles with eye-contact. Making too little is a much bigger problem. At least if someone looks at you a lot you can look away, but if they don't look at all it is difficult to build a relationship.

One of the main reasons for using effective eye-contact as a speaker, a presenter, hosting a meeting or interview, or even if you are just telling a joke or story to friends, is to hold the attention of your listeners.

People will only give you as much attention as you give them. Remember the kids who used to sit on the back row in school, ducking down behind everyone else so they couldn't be seen by the teacher? Were they more or less chatty than the kids on the front row? The same lack of concentration happens unintentionally in meetings, seminars and in groups of friends if they cannot make eye-contact with you, or if you avoid looking at them.

Obviously you must not stare, but when you are speaking aim to make eye-contact with your audience (however many you are speaking to) for about 60% of the time. This may seem quite low to you, however, if you want to be really fluent in your thoughts when you are speaking you will have a natural urge to look away anyway, simply to gather your thoughts.

When you are speaking to people your eye-contact is all about showing them you care about their reaction, gauging how they feel about your ideas and reacting accordingly.

The intricacies of eye-movements and reading other people's expressions and body language take much longer to understand fully, which you can learn more about in our workshops and seminars. For now, just remember that tension and eye-contact are all about creating flexibility in your communication style, because your 'it' factor needs to be fluid and match your situation and the people around you.

One of the best things about eye-contact is simply that it allows you to place your focus outside of yourself, getting rid of what Buddhists call the 'monkey mind'.

The Monkey Mind

Ever had that little voice in your head when you're talking in front of a large group that says. "What are people thinking? Do they like what I'm saying? Are they bored? I'd better shut up soon, I bet they're not interested. I should give up now!"

Most people have that voice. By allowing yourself to focus on the people around you, you will quiet this voice and 'get in the zone' of concentration you want. You'll be self aware rather than self-conscious. You'll have additional confidence and a feeling that everything is flowing well when you need it. Plus you'll have a better understanding and connection with the people around you.

I discovered this once in a classic nightmare situation.

I was giving an after-dinner speech at a conference. I usually insist

to be booked to speak earlier in the day, because after dinner half of the audience have had too much to drink, with all the free alcohol provided at these events, so I have to pay extra attention to entertaining them and capturing their imagination with body language and voice techniques.

About half-way through this speech there was some heckling from the back. Some people don't like this happening as it puts them off. Personally I've grown to love it. It gives me an opportunity to show that I know a lot more about my specialist topic than I've got written down in my script.

"Let me ask you something!" yelled a slurring voice from the back.

"Yes, of course," I replied.

"What makes you think we're even listening to you? You haven't asked us any questions yet!"

"That's an interesting point, sir. Fortunately, I'm a body language specialist, so I have the advantage that I can just look at the audience and understand if they are listening to me or not very quickly. For instance, this lady wearing red in the second row wasn't fully convinced of the value of my speech until after about four minutes, when the tension dropped from her shoulders and forehead. This gentleman over here, four rows back, didn't really want to be here listening to me until I won him over in the congruency exercise, when his shifting stopped and his gaze became more fixed on me. This lady towards the back, wearing blue, wasn't fully convinced until about ten minutes into the speech when her head leaned over to one side and started nodding in rhythm to my words..."

And so it went on.

Eventually, after reciting an analysis I had been making of around a dozen people throughout the room the man realised how important the group's reactions and attention was to me and happily sat back down. He even asked to buy me a drink after we finished.

The real key here is to focus your attention on your audience when you speak, not yourself. They will guide you in what sort of reaction your ideas are getting and how you should continue.

Do you need to clarify what you just said? Are you going too fast or to slow? Are they staring at you in amazement, or bewildered confusion?

This is what eye-contact is all about - making a human connection with people, reading their reactions and responding to them.

You must avoid at all costs what I like to call the "Blue Peter"

THE 'IT' FACTOR **99**

syndrome. This hugely successful children's TV show included lessons in how to make things, from cakes to cardboard castles. Due to the time limits they had, whenever they showed you how to make something they would always finish off by saying, "And here is one I prepared earlier!" as they produced their ready-made finished product.

This is exactly what many people do in important meetings. They create a speech, or think of a joke, or a presentation or sales pitch, then they decide exactly how they are going to say it before they begin, regardless of people's reactions.

They may get a reasonable response from the audience, but it won't be electric. The best comedians will listen to their audience and time their delivery based on the reactions they are getting from people. This ensures that the punch-line of the joke will get as much laughter as possible. The best actors will react to the other actors they are working with and deliver their lines based on what is really happening in the scene at that moment, on that day. It's called 'presence' because that moment-to-moment interaction keeps you fully present.

Great story-tellers, presenters and sales people do exactly the same thing - they do not deliver a script of words they prepared earlier. They read and respond to their audience.

Tim Gallwey is a Harvard graduate and best-selling author since the 1970s, when the first book in 'The Inner Game' series was published. He realised, while working as a tennis coach, that he could dramatically increase the success of his clients by helping them focus outwards, rather than inwards, diminishing the inner voice and getting people into a natural 'zone' of concentration.

He has since applied this to achieving better results in golf, skiing, music, relieving stress and helping people thrive in corporate business.

As he explains, "There is always an inner game being played in your mind no matter what outer game you are playing. How aware you are of this game can make the difference between success and failure in the outer game."

Former President Bill Clinton is described as having the 'it' factor, because when he talks to you it feels like 'you're the most important person in the world to him in that moment'. In the book "The Natural" author Joe Klein describes him as the 'most compelling politician of his generation'.

You can achieve this effect yourself partly from the instinctive reactions generated through your eye-contact and outward focus. For best results with this, you may want to explore Tim Gallwey's books or get some personal coaching, to avoid unusual staring activities, while you improve your skills!

Until then, the main thing I have learnt is that if someone is looking in your direction, with energy in their posture, face or even just their eyes, they are paying attention. So deliver your message whole-heartedly with the skills you are learning here, keep gauging their reaction, and they will keep on listening. If you use your posture, legs and arms to captivate their attention appropriately you will see the results for yourself.

But we still have one further element to discuss. Having introduced you to the other five ingredients it's time to move on to the 'S' in P.L.A.T.E.S™....

"Every time you smile at someone, it is an action of love, a gift to that person, a beautiful thing."

Mother Teresa

CHAPTER 12

Primitive Signals

You may well think that putting 'Smile' in the six key elements of the 'it' factor is a bit basic and, well, 'Disney'. Let's be very clear - if you smile all the time people will think you're on medication! If you save it for just the right moments you can give off a sense of personal warmth, get people to laugh more at your jokes and reach a part of people that most communication signals miss.

Unlike many body language signals, smiling is an inborn, instinctive reaction.

It is the same around the world. Other signals like 'thumbs up', 'come here', nodding your head and pointing are all learnt signals. You watch other people doing them and copy them. They mean different things in different countries. We learn them from the people around us.

Smiling is different. Even a blind baby knows to smile when it is happy. It can also be seen and recognised from a further distance than any other expression.

Smiling (genuinely) at the right time can have a tremendous effect. The main point for this chapter is that when you are nervous, in an important meeting or interaction, you often forget how you would naturally behave. Tension can creep in and limits your movements, limiting your ability to connect fully with people.

To make sure you always perform at your best and achieve the success you want in key moments, here's a quick checklist for crucial times when smiling is most important:

1) Depending on which research you look at, we make a first impression on some one in the first 7-15 seconds we meet. After that point it is difficult to alter their impression of you. They will simply be looking for signs that their initial impression was right.

Remember to smile genuinely in the first few seconds of any interaction if you want to create a sense of personal warmth and affection for the person you are meeting. It is not always appropriate though. For instance, if you are going to fire a member of staff or deliver bad news smiling will set up the wrong tone and expectation of what you are about to say, even if you are simply hoping to lighten the tone.

2) To leave a warm lasting impression at the end of an interaction. As Tony Buzan explains, through his wonderful 'Mind Map' system, the first and last things you do will be the things that people remember the most about you. Memory of an interaction works like a valley, starting at a high peak, dropping rapidly, then rising to a high peak again at the end.

In order to boost people's memory of you during the middle of an interaction you need to create peak emotional experiences, changing the way they FEEL, as explained earlier.

So the first and last things you do are your key 'lasting impressions'.

I'm guessing that you may have thought about these first two before, but what about the next one?

3) Just before a joke or light-hearted comment, to let people know that it is okay for them to laugh. People are afraid of laughing at an inappropriate moment, so if you are always serious with them, or if you look tense, they will be uncertain whether they should laugh or not.

If you then unexpectedly crack a joke it will be met with uneasy silence. Smiling shortly before lets people know what sort of tone your comment is intended to have and how they should react. When you are speaking it's your job to set the tone and let the listener feel comfortable in your presence, another essential part of the 'it' factor.

This doesn't mean that you roll around the floor with tears of laughter before or during your own joke. If you do you'll kill it - all of the required laughter will have been done by you. People will just look at you strangely, rather than listen to what you are saying. Remember, the point of body language is to serve your words, not distract from them.

Just give the audience a hint of the tone required, in the same way that a news reader will never cry at a sad story, they will just have a serious expression and voice to let you know the tone of the story and guide your response. They then change their tone right at the beginning of the next story, letting you know how you should feel about it in advance.

Have you ever had a conversation with someone that went a bit like this one…

"What do you think of this?" they ask you.

"Oh yes, very nice," you reply, just trying to be agreeable.

"Really? Well, I hate it…"

This is a great example of someone trying to be nice and give the right response to their friend, but if there is no real guidance for where the story or conversation is going you have no clue how to react! We often wait, poised to find out if we are supposed to be impressed, celebrating or commiserating. It's up to you to let people know, making them feel safe that they have reacted in the way you wanted, allowing them to maintain rapport with you.

Suppose a woman says to you, *"I'm pregnant"*. How do you respond? She could be overjoyed, miserable or scared. What should you say to her? What does she need to hear from you? *"Congratulations!"* or *"Don't worry, it's all going to be fine"*. The only way to tell is to look at her expression. If you can't tell from that then you need to ask her how she feels.

My wife is a Doctor, seeing 30-40 different patients a day, five days per week. Of those who are pregnant some are elated, some scared, uncertain, ambivalent, suicidal, overjoyed or bewildered. Simply knowing their condition isn't enough to know how to proceed.

Words are facts. How we feel about those facts, and how people react, will be determined by your body language and tone of voice.

If you are talking to a large group they can't ask you how they are supposed to respond. You have to show them.

Smiling doesn't always need to include using your mouth or showing your teeth, as few great comedians do this during a joke. A smile in the eyes is more effective for signalling a laughter moment (and easier to recover from if people don't get the joke - there is nothing lonelier than smiling and laughing at your own joke when nobody else does!).

To create a warm impression on people, a smile at the beginning and at the end of a meeting will do wonders, if it is genuine. The rest of the time you can go into business mode without fear of looking cold. Start by setting the tone then focus on your content.

This brings us to the end of our six key elements of body language. These may seem simple, but they are by far the most common areas that people around the world most need to improve.

If you master these areas you will excel in your everyday interactions and be far better equipped than the thousands of people I have had the opportunity to coach and study over the last 14 years.

The main thing to beware of is complacency. A gentleman who was sent on my training session a few years ago told me that he felt patronised by the content of my session as he 'already knew them'. Unfortunately, he was unaware that he never bothered to use them. After our discussion, I then watched him stand up in front of 20 people to run his own training session, as he paced back and forth, looking at the ground, with his hands clenched together and his face full of tension. He failed to use any of the techniques

I had spoken about. He felt he didn't need them. The audience shifted uneasily in their seats as he quickly alienated them and threw away any sense of rapport or authority he could have had.

His content was actually brilliant, as I began to realise when I heard it for the tenth time on a long project we were both working on. He was highly knowledgeable. But I watched group after group lose interest. The feedback forms we used reflected this.

People didn't seem to listen, care about or remember his section. Like a plain, old box hidden behind the Christmas tree, nobody knew of all the wonders he had within as his personal presentation didn't capture their interest enough to discover the treasures inside.

The 'it' factor, in essence, is about taking all the wonderful stuff you have to offer the world and presenting it in a way that people will appreciate it, admire it and want more of it.

These six key elements are simple to use and practise. So make sure you do, because changing just one inch of your body language will transform the personal impact you make on the people around you every day. By doing so you will be able to reach your full potential and the level of success you deserve.

It may not seem like you're making a massive change, but the 'it' factor is about the little things that make a big difference. As simplistic as it may sound, all it takes is a little bit extra to go from ordinary to extraordinary.

"Beneath the make-up and behind the smile, I'm just a girl who wishes for the world."

Marilyn Monroe

CHAPTER 13

Walking The Talk

The 'it' factor in action

I watched a stock-market guru giving a presentation, trying to sell his trading ideas to a large room of people. He said his ideas were fool-proof and anyone could be a millionaire using his techniques with no prior experience, or even being good at maths.

Quite a claim.

His audience were complete novices to the stock market, as you might expect with the claims he was making. They really wanted to learn. They were a totally captive audience.

Until he lost them.

He began by marching about the stage, while showing pictures of him doing amazing things up on the screen, like flying a jet-fighter plane and climbing Everest. His body looked macho, like Tarzan, but when he spoke he was breathy and squeaky. He was tense and his breathing very shallow, cutting off his natural resonance. His voice didn't sound the way you expected it to when you looked at him. His personal 'packaging' and the 'contents' were mis-matched. He lacked congruency.

People were still interested though. They still desperately wanted to learn. They were prepared to ignore this distraction to listen to his words of wisdom.

In his panic of feeling nervous about being in front of a large group, something in his mind flicked to fast-forward. A set of power-point slides came up on the screen that was full of complex stock market graphs, figures, charts and calculations. Due to his nerves he started talking through the information far too quickly. He was losing the novices he had promised to make rich. They needed him to be slow, calm and reassuring.

They needed to feel that it was all as easy as he promised.

All they saw was a flustered panic - not a great advert for stress-free trading!

As he looked at his audience I got the sense he knew he was

losing their attention. He looked back at his screen and said something like, "Okay I know it looks complex, but it's really not," before he went on to the next slide. It looked equally daunting. Instead of talking the audience calmly through this one, he rushed it again.

He got progressively quicker and breathier as he went on. He made stock market trading look like harder work than running a marathon. By the end the audience was numb from the machine-gun speed of his words and slides.

If he had just slowed down and considered how he wanted the audience to feel, he could have made a huge success of the event. The content was good. The delivery wasn't. He fell short of his desired reaction.

The next speaker came on, with similar 'get rich quick' advice, but in contrast this guy looked as if he was strolling along the beach. He spoke cheerfully, standing centred, with flowing gestures. At the end he offered people the chance to learn more about his money-making techniques, then said, "it was nice chatting with you all" and left.

That statement said it all. While the first guy had been over-whelming the audience with power, talking at us, the second felt he was merely chatting with the 700 people who watched. At the back of the room, squeaky Tarzan's stall was deserted. Everyone was flocking to the other man who had showed that life could be a beach, by embodying the feeling he wanted us all to have. His credentials were far lower, but he had 'it'. In making an important investment decision, the 700 people in the audience made a judgement based on emotion, not logic. As Coca Cola used to tell us, 'you can't beat the feeling'.

It's not just individuals who make decisions based on gut reaction.

Big companies do this every day.

In a 'credit crunch', logic tells a company that they are losing money, but emotions will make them decide what to do about it.

Fear will make them sack brilliant members of staff, to save money. Faith will make them invest more money in training their staff to improve the company's fortunes. They will never admit that the decision is based on emotion, they will just give their share-holders a list of "logical reasons" for what is in fact an emotional response. Even if they hated making that choice they would do so because they wanted to please their boss, pay their mortgage, silence their critics or satisfy any other type of emotional catalyst.

You have now been introduced to some of the methods available to ensure you engage people's feelings more effectively, to help you achieve a new level of success (although I'm sure you appreciate these are just some of the highlights) - a more diverse range of techniques are available, with more depth and detail to help you succeed, if you want to get in touch with us directly, now that you're familiar with the essential foundation concepts.

So far you have learnt the initial steps of how to...

• Master your personal impact with your P.L.A.T.E.S™

• Avoid becoming a 'push-over' and boost your natural presence, with a strong 'centred' position

• Change the way you feel with your body language

• Show certainty and authority with 'Palms Down'

• Be open and welcoming with 'Palms Up'

• Re-gain your natural charisma, through congruency and releasing unnecessary tension

This is all great progress. If you use all the skills we have covered so far then you will certainly earn people's attention.

But.

You will still have the challenge of how to hold people's attention.

Everyone can be interesting for 30 seconds. After that we begin to lose interest, if everything you are doing is the same. We live in an 'MTV generation' where people are used to getting a lot more fast-moving visual stimulation than they would have had 50 years ago.

To ensure absolute success there is one last secret that pulls all of these techniques together to ensure you are confident, congruent and compelling enough to hold their interest...

Passion with precision

Behind every technique I have been sharing with you there must always be a sense of human truth. People buy people so the saying goes, and it's true.

You must use each technique with passion and a sense of real purpose behind it otherwise it just won't work. It will seem false and empty. We all have the passion to express our ideas. Passion by itself isn't enough. We see misguided passion on shows like 'Britain's Got Talent' all the time.

The skills in this book show you how to focus your passion and present it more effectively. The 'it' factor is similar to Federal Express — it will guarantee a fast, effective delivery to your destination, but it's up to you to make sure the content is worthwhile receiving. Sadly, for most people, they have great content (words, ideas, value to offer the world) they just don't know how to deliver it.

That's actually why my study of the 'it' factor began...

The day I started searching for 'it'

When I was 17 my closest friend was the most intelligent, hard-working, diligent, polite and earnest young man you could ever meet. A dignified and talented gentleman, if ever you saw one.

He had earned an 'A' grade in every test and exam I can remember him taking, and he deserved it too.

He applied to Oxford University. He passed their entrance exams with ease. He was invited for an interview.

I got him a good-luck card, as I knew it was his life-long dream to go there. On the envelope I wrote " *If you can't get in, no one can!*"

I still remember the look on his face when I gave it to him.

He shrugged.

> "*I didn't get in.*"

I had no idea what to say. I was stunned.

He told me that he had received a letter that morning telling him that based on his interview and communication skills he had been turned down.

In that moment I knew two things for sure:

1)   Oxford University had missed out on having possibly the most dedicated, intelligent and decent young man they could ever have accepted, based on a fleeting meeting with him.

2)   I would never be as intelligent or hard-working as him, so if I wanted to succeed in life I was going to have to learn what 'it' was that made all the difference between success and failure in a crucial life-changing moment, so that if I was ever given an interview by anybody I would stand a chance at succeeding.

As with everything in life, your CV or credentials may get you through the door, but no further. The rest is up to you.

Little did I realise that in my journey to study 'it' I would stumble upon something that would have the potential to create a much more significant impact for our clients.

A gentleman who attended one of our open workshops in London a couple of years ago appeared very depressed and negative about himself. By the end of the course we had made a huge improvement on his business communication skills, but I wondered how much of it he would use and apply into everyday life.

I bumped into him six months later at a speech I was giving. He seemed so different in the way he was talking to the people around him that I thought it might be his brother or cousin. He came over to talk to me.

> *"Richard, it's great to see you again, I'm looking forward to your speech tonight!"* he said.

> *"Well, I'm sure it's all information that you heard from me last time."*

> *"I certainly hope so. I didn't tell you before, but I was diagnosed with having clinical depression for 16 years before I came on your course. I decided to use the training and the communication techniques as a springboard to change all that. And it worked. I've been behaving differently and people have treated me differently as a result, which has changed how I feel about myself and what I can do."*

I had never realised until then how big the knock-on effects are of applying these skills into your everyday life. Just by making small changes in his body language he had changed the message he was giving to people about who he was, how they should interact with him and how confident he felt.

When you present a different version of yourself people will of course start to treat you differently, which means that you will then feel even better. People will notice this then react even better towards you. And so it goes on, as a self-fulfilling cycle, giving you natural momentum towards your goals.

Whatever impact you want to have in business, or your personal life, I encourage you to start making changes towards it now. It will feel strange at first, as you step outside your past comfort zone of communication, because your style is so intrinsically linked to your identity. However, when you make the shifts recommended here, which have been proven to create success for many people before you, you may be surprised by the results you get and how quickly you get them, in your business and your personal life.

You may have previously thought that your body language was just a by-product of your feelings. You may have thought it was all just natural, instinctive and simply about 'folding your arms'. Hopefully, by being introduced to the finer areas of non-verbal communication, you now understand how important these elements are to your experience of life every day. As shown by the studies conducted by Dr. Paul Ekman over the last forty years, your body language isn't simply a result of how you feel. It works both ways.

You can take control of how people feel about you. Indeed you can take control of how you feel about yourself. If you decide how to behave, adjusting your communication style, body language and use of facial expressions, you can actually determine how you feel and how the people around you feel and respond towards you too, potentially changing the course your life takes in crucial moments.

So choose your P.L.A.T.E.S™ carefully, so that you make the most of everything you have to offer and deliver it in the most effective way.

It may take a while to get the hang of it, and may require further coaching, but it'll be worth it. If you apply these techniques you can transform your life experience and results, just by expressing yourself differently.

As you develop your personal 'it' factor you'll understand that what you really have is a one-way 'express' ticket to take the journey from where you are now to where you want to be.

Enjoy the ride and create your impact.

"Continuous effort – not strength or intelligence – is the key to unlocking our potential."

Winston Churchill

References & Recommended Reading

I owe a huge thanks to the research and studies in this area that have been published by the following people:

1. Richard van de Lagemaat, the author of the "Theory of Knowledge" (published by Cambridge University press). Richard has more than 20 years experience in international education and it was a pleasure to meet him.

2. Dan Ariely, author of 'Predictably Irrational', is a visiting Professor at MIT. His book is an excellent insight into the reality of irrational human behavior and the small things that affect your decisions every day.

3. Dr Howard S. Friedman is a distinguished Professor of Psychology and the Editor of the 'Journal of Nonverbal Behavior'. His research on nonverbal expressiveness and personal charisma has been widely applied in leadership training, medical education, and viral marketing.

4. Malcolm Gladwell's international best-selling books 'Blink' and 'The Tipping Point' are essential reading to understand how small things can make a big difference and change the world we live in.

5. Dr. Paul Ekman is considered one of the Top 100 most eminent psychologists of the 20th Century, and a true master of human emotion. The 'deception detective' Cal Lightman, of the FOX TV series 'Lie To Me', is loosely based on him. His greatest books include 'Emotions Revealed'. He is a living legend in the area of 'reading people'.

6. Tim Gallwey is the author of 'The Inner Game' series of books. His discoveries in performance psychology will help you perform at your very best when you need to. His books include specialist work on improving your game in tennis, golf, work and music.

7. Desmond Morris's book 'Peoplewatching' is the definitive book on body language. If you are serious about learning these skills this is the best book of research I have found on the subject. Many other books are available but his is the original and best 'Body Language Bible'.

Notes

Would you like to learn more?

The three most popular options you may like to book are:

- **Speeches** – Our speeches are very popular at conferences and staff meetings. They are filled with practical tips that will leave your group inspired, entertained and motivated, ready to use new skills back at work.

- **Workshops** – Coaching for a small group of your staff. This will boost your results in sales, negotiations and presentations. There will be plenty of time for personal feedback, giving you immediate and long lasting results. We will always tailor this session to achieve your goals.

- **Personal Coaching** – A personal session with us will ensure you succeed at an important event, such as a speech, interview, or an important meeting.

Our clients include the **UK Parliament, international celebrities** and global corporations such as **IBM & KPMG**, so you can be assured we will give you the very best results.

Don't just take our word for it! This is what our clients say about us...

"**Most training is dry and corporate. What we really need is practical techniques we feel passionate and energised by, that we can take back into the business. With this training you really feel that! The knowledge and passion of the trainers is fantastic!**" –
Dave Askew, BT Group

Conference Speeches

Walk The Talk! – One or Two hours (our most popular option)

Do you want to have more authority, confidence & be more persuasive? These skills instantly boost your results in meetings, sales & presentations. This session is highly interactive, keeping everyone engaged and entertained, with practical skills and motivation your staff will all benefit from.

The Body Talk Secret Signals – One hour
(great as a follow-up speech after 'Walk The Talk')

Increase your success in sales and negotiations by learning to read advanced body talk signals. Discover the subtle moves that reveal hidden thoughts and experience a live lie detection competition with video analysis and champagne prizes, to excite and entertain your audience, as they learn new skills!

Workshops

Personal Influence & Persuasion Skills

If you've ever wondered how to apply the persuasion and influencing skills of Paul McKenna and Derren Brown to business - this is your chance to find out how it's done! You will experience unforgettable demonstrations, plus master the essential body talk principles of selling! This is a lively and entertaining session, with plenty of simple techniques, which sales people of all levels will enjoy and gain new skills from.

One or Two Day Workshops – Powerful Presentations

You can have up to twelve staff coached by two expert trainers, giving them the skills they need to have presence, confidence and be really engaging when they present.

On the 2-day course you learn to apply all these skills to sales, negotiations and networking, giving you the full package to boost the success of your business. It includes a Before & After DVD of each delegate, personal development plans and long lasting improvements for all involved.

You may also like to book one of the following workshops for your team:

- **Personal Impact:** win respect and rapport with clients and colleagues
- **Media skills:** for successful TV, radio and press interviews
- **Outstanding Customer Service:** Give your team The 'It' Factor
- **International body language:** Develop stronger business relationships
- **Business Leaders:** Advanced communication skills for success

You can reach us at:

UK Body Talk Ltd.
121 Standard Road
Hounslow, TW4 7AY
United Kingdom
Email: info@ukbodytalk.com
Tel: 0044 (0)8451 30 70 99

Contact us today and find out more about how we can help you. We look forward to hearing from you and working with you soon!